MW01110092

Learn t

By Ed Drury

Acknowledgments

Cover art by Star4mation. There are several people who have contributed to this booklet. I would like to thank just a few: Eric Dash, Leo Franz and Will Hathaway of the Multnomah Arts Center for encouraging me to start didjeridu classes in my local community; Brian Pertl for teaching me how to teach and providing a role model for all of us; Frank Coppieters for his wonderful sacred sound explorations; My wonderful wife Lisa for her patience, love and support; all my students who have taught me much more than they could know; John Paul Barrett, without whose editing this book would contain many more mistakes than it does; and most important, the inventors of the didjeridu - the first Australians.

Introduction

The didjeridu is an Australian Aboriginal musical instrument. Traditionally, it was only known in Eastern Kimberly and the northern third of the Northern Territory of Australia. It is made from a hollowed piece of bamboo or wood, about four or five feet long, and a mouthpiece made from bees wax or hardened gum. The player blows the instrument much like one plays the tuba. The precision and variety of rhythm produced on the didjeridu are very striking. Sometimes it sounds like a deep organ stop being played continuously. At other times like a drum beaten in three-four time, varying according to the type of song and dance it is accompanying. The continuous nature of the sound is most remarkable. This is accomplished by a technique known as "circular breathing."

Non-aboriginal people first documented encountering the didjeridu when an explorer named T.B. Wilson described an aboriginal man playing an instrument called the eboro in Raffles Bay on the Coburg Peninsula in 1835. He described the instrument as being made of bamboo and about three feet in length. The earliest references to the instrument all occur in the later part of the nineteenth century. In the century that followed, the instrument was observed by anthropologists on mainland Arnhem Land. The hard wood instruments particular to Arnhem Land (yirdakis) were usually crafted from eucalyptus species like "stringy bark" and "woolybutt" in the North, and Red River Gum further south near Katherine. There is also documentation of didjeridus made of palm even further south. By the time anthropologist Alice Moyle was publishing her field work in the mid 1970s, aboriginal groups where using found pipes such as land rover tailpipes and water pipes as didjeridus.

Information about the didjeridu and the music to which it belonged began spreading to the outside world through the published accounts of anthropologists. This was the start of a separation of the use of the instrument from the cultural setting to which it owes its invention. It started in the mid part of the last century and continues through present day. But the anthropologists where documenting the music through recordings, transcriptions of music and descriptive prose.

In 1974 Prof. AP Elkin would write, "From 1927 on I had seen corroborees with their singing and dancing... but it was not until I made a survey in 1946, almost around Arnhem Land, that I realized the vitality and richness of the singing and dancing of that region. I therefore determined to make permanent records as soon as possible, so that musicians and dancers would be able to hear and see this part of Aboriginal culture, even if only at second hand."

The didjeridu, as recently as 100 years ago, had a restricted distribution in Australia. Earlier researchers such as Elkin (1938) noted that it was "only known in Eastern Kimberley and the northern third of the Northern Territory". Although now played around the globe, traditional playing style and technique is confined to this region. A tremendous body of documentation resulted from these studies which included descriptive texts, field recordings and musical transcriptions. This work continues today revealing subtle changes in the instrument's distribution, influences from current events and recording technology which has improved dramatically since the early days. Field recordings were made commercially available and drew interest from a broader audience, but a lot of the attention focused on the instrument known as the didjeridu rather than the musical and cultural context it was in.

The recordings often featured demonstrations of the sounds and rhythms of the didjeridu rather than its role as an accompaniment. Intended to showcase the instrument's range of harmonics and rhythmic accuracy, often these demonstrations (or solos) where mistaken to be traditional works by listeners. The notion of the didjeridu as an instrument of self expression began forming in western minds. Traditionally, a typical performance will consist of one or more singers (one of whom is the lead songman), each with a pair of sticks or something else percussive (at times makeshift) and one didjeriduist. Some genres of music do not use didjeridu, but where used, only one is ever played at a time. If for some reason a didjeriduist is unavailable, the piece can still be performed.

Until recently, the didjeridu was little known outside Australia. Today, its popularity has spread around the world. Traditionally, the instrument was "tuned" to the lead song man's voice. But today, many didjeridus are tuned to concert pitches in order to be played with contemporary instruments. Its distinctive sound can be heard in rock bands, Celtic groups, new age recordings, movies and television commercials. A skilled player can obtain a rich variety of overtones, harmonics and voicings that make the sound of the didjeridu unique.

The Yothu Yindi Foundation, in a 1999 newsletter, eloquently expressed an Aboriginal perspective on the issue of appropriation of the instrument. "...Yet Yolngu people are concerned that the emergence of a global culture and the commercialization of the Yidaki [sic] has the potential to separate the Yidaki from its origins in the sacred stories which are at the heart of the songs. Ritual leaders of northeast Arnhem Land are calling for a new relationship with Balanda which recognizes the centrality of the Yidaki to the Aboriginal groups who by right and tradition have the Yidaki as one of the instruments of cultural expression." (Yothu Yindi Foundation Newsletter 1999)

Leran to Play the Didjeridu

Chapter One First Lesson

1.1. The basic drone

Puff out your cheeks and push out your lips, drawing the corners of your mouth back a bit, allowing the center part of your lips to be loose. Blow air through your lips, allowing them to vibrate, making a low pitched buzzing sound. Now transfer this loose lip buzzing technique to the mouthpiece of the didjeridu. There are two styles : straight on with the mouthpiece centered on the lips below the nose, or to the right or left of center. Both methods are acceptable, just use whichever seems natural to you. Never press the mouthpiece tightly against your lips as this interferes with the buzzing of the lips and will case the lips to become sore after playing in a short amount of time. Take a deep breath in through your nose and blow evenly down the didjeridu while buzzing your lips. If the sound is high pitched (e.g. a trumpet note) relax your lips a little so they vibrate at a lower rate. If your note sounds flat and weak, try blowing a little harder.

For your first exercise with the basic drone I recommend this exercise as not only a great way to improve your tone and breath control, but a good warm up exercise for each practice session: Play the basic drone until you run out of air. Do not move the mouthpiece away from your lips when you run out of air, but instead, take a nice full breath in through your nose. Play the drone again, this time trying to make the tone last a little longer. Repeat this process again and again until you can sustain the drone approximately twenty seconds or more. The longer the better. Each time, try to make each note not only last a bit longer than the previous note, but sound steadier and clearer. This exercise will improve the sound quality of your basic drone, but increase your breath control.

1.2. Creating your first rhythms -

Gut Slaps -

Our first rhythm is a basic 4/4 beat produced by bouncing the air through our buzzing lips using the tummy muscles just as if we were expelling a deep belly laugh (e.g. - ha!ha!ha!ha!). Using the diaphragm while playing the didjeridu is important. As the strongest respiratory muscle it can supply the largest amount of volume for the least amount of work. One of the primary health benefits of playing the didjeridu involves the use of this muscle. So breathe deeply and feel the beat!

Tongue - Next, try producing the same rhythm using the tongue by mouthing the word "Tu-Tu-Tu-Tu." The tip of the tongue is placed just behind the upper front teeth and as quickly snapped downward. Variations of this sound can be made by mouthing the word "Da-Da-Da-Da" or the word "Ta-Ta-Ta-Ta."

Cheeks -

By squeezing the cheeks we can change the harmonics of the sound of the didjeridu. Playing the basic drone, allow your cheeks to puff out, then squeeze the cheeks together slowly lettting them puff out again. A "wah-wah" effect should result. Think of a bellows squeezing in and out. Practice doing this slowly at first and then faster. Finally, vary the speed by doing two slow cheek squeezes followed by three faster ones. (2-3 beat). Add further variations as you master the technique of cheek squeezing.

1.3. Circular Breathing -

A) It is helpful to do some strengthening exercises. Droning while squeezing the cheeks as described above will help. Another exercise is to alternately puff your cheeks out and squeeze them in forcefully. Start with one minute of this exercise and work up to 3 minutes.

B) Timing. Puff out your cheeks and use your lips to make a small opening in the center of your mouth as if blowing into a straw. Try to make a small steady stream of air come out of this opening using only the air in your cheeks. By placing the palm of your hand in front of your lips you should be able to feel the air stream. Breathe in through your nose while you are squeezing the air in your cheeks out.

C) Transfer the previous step to the didjeridu. Try to allow your lips to vibrate loosely so a low short tone is produced. It should sound something like "harrumph." Now blow the air in your lungs through your lips, letting them vibrate as in the basic drone. Allow your cheeks to puff out as you run out of air, and then repeat the process from the beginning.

D) Continue working with step C, increasing the speed such that the pause between the sound emitted by your cheek squeeze and the sound of your basic drone decreases. Don't worry about the transfer between the cheek powered sound and the lung powered drone being smooth for now. It will come with practice. Just try to keep shortening the pause until it disappears completely.

E) To work on smoother transfers between air coming from your cheeks and air coming from your lungs, place a straw in a glass of water. The glass should be only about a third full. Alternating cheek-squeezing with a sniff of air through the nose and blowing, try to keep a steady stream of bubbles coming from the end of the straw - breathing in while you squeeze your cheeks. If you can keep the bubbles going smoothly without pause, you are circular breathing.

Important Points in Lesson One

1. It is a common mistake, especially when attempting new skills, to press the mouthpiece tightly against the lips. Stay relaxed and use just enough pressure to assure a seal.

2. Do not over practice. If your cheek muscles or lips become sore, you are over using them. The best results are obtained by daily practice. Fifteen minutes per day is a good starting point, but practice time is highly individual. Seek a level that you can fit into your daily routine.

3. Circular breathing is a rhythm. Many people try to set a rhythm and fit the breathing to the rhythm. A better approach is to create a rhythm around the breaths. Breath the rhythm! Different rhythms require varying amounts of air. Start with simple rhythms based on an even beat. Then experiment with different tempos. Finally, work on more complex rhythms.

4. Though some people learn the basic skills of circular breathing rather quickly, most take some time. There is no correlation between how long it takes you to learn a new skill and how good a player you may eventually become. There is a lot more to playing and enjoying the didjeridu than circular breathing. Be patient with yourself and realize that these are skills that can be learned and practiced. They are not the insights of mystics handed down through a select lineage.

5. Your goal should be self expression. Work to play your music. In the lessons, you are just getting the basic tools. You are both musician and instrument when you play the didjeridu. Choosing to play is a step you took for yourself, everything else will fall into place.

Chapter Two Second Lesson

2.1. Harmonics -

All sounds are composed of harmonics. To realize this, sing a single note and mouth the vowel sound "E" then, without changing notes, make the vowel sound "O." Although you are singing the same note, the vowel sound "E" emphasizes the upper harmonics and sounds quite different from the vowel sound "O."

A) Playing the basic drone, mouth the vowels sound "E", then shape your mouth as if your were saying the word "Oh." Notice the harmonic fall? As you go from "E" to "O" the harmonics shift or "fall" from high to low. Obviously, you can do a harmonic rise by starting with the sound "O" and moving to the sound "E" with your mouth. This transition can be smoothed out a bit by adding the mouth shape "A" between the "E" and "O" sounds. Finally, experiment with all the vowel sounds (a,e,i,o and u) .

B) Careful lip shaping can also affect the harmonics of the didjeridu. By altering the shape of the opening between your two buzzing lips, much as in whistling, you can create a variable upper harmonic sound. Likewise, cheek and tongue positioning in combination with mouth shaping can add a wide variety of rich harmonic tones to the didjeridu. These are worth a great deal of attention, as each didjeridu will respond a bit differently to these maneuvers.

C) As you can now see, any vowel or consonant sound which you can enunciate will affect the harmonics of the didjeridu. It's now a small step to articulate syllables. Try mouthing the syllable "did". Follow that with the syllable "jer."

D) By taking a word like didjeridu, and breaking it up into distinct syllables who's order can be varied, a wide variety of musical rhythms can be improvised. For example, "did-did-did-ger-ree, did-did-doo" will make a nicely varied little rhythm. A practice rhythm which I enjoy comes from a very popular song, "do-wah-diddy-diddy-dum-diddy-doo."

2.2. Voicings -

By using the vocal chords while playing the basic drone, various effects can be added. There are two basic categories : a) animal or bird imitations, and b) singing or humming various notes.

A) While playing the basic drone, try making a sound like a dog barking with your vocal chords. If you find it a bit difficult to do, practice in front of a mirror without the didjeridu. Make a sound like "woof woof woof" without moving your lips. Any sound you can make without moving your lips can be used while playing the didjeridu.

B) Singing distinct or indistinct notes while droning adds a rich texture to the total effect. Specific notes will vary according to the pitch of the didjeridu and the vocal range of the player. I find a good harmony to strive for is a fifth above the dominant note of the didjeridu. This would be a G for a didjeridu which plays a C. It is good, I feel, for a player to know what pitch his or her didjeridu plays. If you have a keyboard available, you should be able to find the pitch your instrument plays in by playing a flat droning note on the didjeridu while experimenting with the notes found two octaves below middle C on the piano. Frequency analyzers are great, but when trying to read the output, be sure to play a simple droning note without harmonics (i.e.- tongue flat on the floor of the mouth and cheeks stationary). Otherwise the output of the frequency analyzer will vary wildly and may be misleading.

C) A good effect, when doing vocals, is to vary the volume of your voice in relation to the didjeridu. This takes a bit of practice, but it will make all your voicings much more interesting to the listener.

D) To the aboriginals, the animals and birds of Australia figure prominently in their rituals and songs. The Kookaburra call, in particular, is much loved. Its comical call is often imitated with a musical laugh through the didjeridu. Other times, it is imitated by using the back of the tongue against the roof of the mouth as in pronouncing the letter "K" and varying the pitch of the voice up, then down and finally back up a scale. Frogs are easily imitated by making a croaking sound. I generally say the word "rib-it" in a low voice to imitate the frog. The bush pigeon is similar to a dove and makes a cooing sound.

As entertaining as these imitations are, it is often equally effective to imitate animals which reside in the player's own country. In the pacific northwest, for example, there is an abundant variety of birds whose calls may be emulated. From the prosaic crow or raven to the more esoteric hoot of an owl, learning to imitate birds and animals with which you are familiar is challenging and rewarding.

2.3. Bounced Breaths -

There is another, more rhythmic, way to circular breath. Go back to lesson one and review our first rhythm which was accomplished with gut slaps. What we want to do here is bounce the air through our buzzing lips and snatch a quick sniff of air through the nose immediately after. It is helpful to start out by pairing two gut slaps close together. "Haha!", with the sniff of air coming right after the second gut slap. Once you have the basic principle, you can vary the number of gut slaps (and therefore the rhythm) to breaths from 1:1 to 3:1 and so on.

Important Points in Lesson Two

1. When using mouth shaping to create harmonics, exaggerate every syllable to accent the effect you're trying to achieve.

2. Varying the relative volume of vocalizations adds another dimension to their sound.

3. Both mouth shaping and vocals can be practiced away from the didjeridu.

4. When attempting bounced breaths, make your breath just a short sniff of air. Vary the number of bounces per breath to vary the rhythm and tempo.

Chapter Three Third Lesson

3.1 Special Effects -

Numerous sound effects can be obtained while playing the didjeridu using the tongue, cheeks and jaw.

A) Tongue Slaps -

By rapidly bringing the tongue from the back of the mouth to the front of the mouth and back again, a sound similar to a bubble bursting may be created. Your tongue should actually slam against the back of your teeth and be quickly withdrawn. Some practice is required to prevent the tongue from completely blocking air flow and interrupting the buzzing of your lips.

B) Cheek Slaps or Expulsions -

While playing the basic drone, let your cheeks puff out. Sharply, contract both cheeks as if your were blowing a spit wad out of a straw. If done with enough force, this will result in a sound which can be described as, "whap!". Next try this same technique using only one cheek. Using one cheek, you may discover that the sound created is sharper. Rapidly repeated cheek slaps are an oft heard effect on many non-traditional didjeridu recordings.

C) Jaw drops

While playing the basic drone, drop the jaw downward parting the front teeth and then return it to the normal position. You should hear the drone drop in pitch and then return to it's previous note. This technique allows you to "bend " the note. Either the drop or rise of the jaw may be varied in speed to emphasize the tonal effect.

During the jaw rise, air is squeezed out of the oral cavity. As a result, you can sniff air in through the nose during the jaw rise, providing another method of circular breathing.

3.2. Adding vocals to special effects -

To add another dimension to tongue slaps, cheek expulsions and jaw drops, experiment with using your vocal chords to voice different pitches during the maneuver. A good example would be to sing a high note and make it fall while moving the jaw upwards such that the pitch of the basic drone is rising while the pitch of your voice is falling.

3.3. Overtones -

Overtones are the result of increasing the frequency of the buzzing lips by tightening them as is done in playing brass instruments like the trumpet or French horn. Play the basic drone and tighten up your lips while slightly increasing the air flow through them. This should result in a note whose pitch is approximately a tenth above the dominant. Now practice going from the basic drone to the overtone note and back to the basic drone. With some practice, you should be able to move between the two notes smoothly. Start slowly and gradually try and make the overtone note as brief as possible.

Another method of producing the first overtone note is accomplished by emphatically pronouncing the word, "two" while simultaneously jetting out a burst of air. This produces a dramatic rhythmic "tooting" sound which can be used to emphasize various rhythms.

With some practice, many people find that they can create second and even third overtone notes. In traditional aboriginal playing, however, only the first overtone note has ever been documented to my knowledge.

3.4. Putting some things together -

Once a few simple tools have been practiced, the fun starts! There are an infinite number of approaches to creating music using the didjeridu and the ones you choose to express yourself with are going to depend on setting, mood and personal preferences. As an example, let's create a phrase composed of syllables and make that phrase the basic underlying rhythm. For the sake of simplicity, let's make this a repetitive rhythm. We will simply try to keep the same rhythmic phrase going and add layers of effects to it. Because we want to try to keep the phrase going continuously, we should account for a circular breath in our phrase.

First , we will assign some names to the sounds that circular breaths make. A breath taken during a cheek squeeze could be called , "Wah." Let's call a breath taken during a gut slap, "Ah Huh" (see "bounced breaths"). Finally, let's assign the phrase , "ah hah" to breaths taken during the rise of the jaw after a jaw drop.

Let's make our first composition very basic. We'll start with the rhythm, "did-ee-wah-did-ee-did-ee." In other words, mouth the phrase, "Did-ee", take a circular breath and mouth the same phrase again twice. Repeat this and you find you have a breath every three "diddies"! Since the breaths come so often, we can avoid becoming over inflated by taking small quick snatches of air each time we squeeze the cheeks.

Once we have the basic rhythm going we can add a little texture to the phrase "did-ee" , by actually saying it using our vocal chords. You can use a high falsetto, a normal speaking voice, a lower tone, or vary the voice each time. You can add more interest to the piece by only using your vocal chords every second or third time through the phrase.

Now do the same phrase, but this time play it through twice and on the third time skip the phrase and put in a laughing kookaburra. After the kookaburra sings his comical morning greeting, return to playing the phrase. You might find that you run out of air before you can complete the kookaburra laugh! While playing the didjeridu, our goal is to keep our requirements for oxygen and need to exhale carbon dioxide in balance. With a little practice, you will be able to take the appropriate size breaths for any given rhythm. Then it is a matter of adjusting this breaths to the task at hand. Just prior to doing vocalizations, take in a little more air with your circular breaths. You may also need to increase the volume of your circular breaths for an interval just after a vocalization or any special effects.

3.5. Roots of rhythms -

All life has rhythm. Breathing itself is a rhythm. I want to suggest a couple of exercises to help you find sources for rhythms. The only requirement is to open your senses. Some rhythms are heard. For an example, the spin cycle of my washing machine beats out some nice variations in 4/4 time! I can sit and play the didjeridu while my clothes are spinning out all the dirt and grime - a real cleansing of mind and body covering. Are there rhythms around your house that you can learn to accompany? Some rhythms come to us through emotions. The rapid pulse of physical attraction, the slow pulse of quiet reflection, and the lonely rhythms of various sad times are all part of a greater cycle. Through music, we have a voice to give to all of our feelings.

Important Points in Lesson Three

1. When practicing special effects like tongue slaps, cheek expulsions and jaw drops, remember to keep gentle pressure against the mouthpiece. The tendency, especially for beginners, is to press the mouthpiece harder against the mouth when doing unusual maneuvers. The same gentle pressure that was discussed in lesson one is all that is required.

2. When adding vocalizations to special effects, experiment with a wide variety of pitches and volumes relative to the didjeridu to discover what works best for you.

3. Overtones may take quite a bit of practice. The irony is that they are most effective when used sparingly and the overtone note is very brief. The overtone note takes a bit more air to support the higher frequency of lip buzzing required. Try to give the overtone note the amount of air required and no more. In most forms of traditional playing that use the overtone, it is subtle indeed. Try to avoid a honking sound, but strive instead for a clear bell like note.

4. For your first didjeridu compositions, it is probably best to start with simple rhythms based on word phrases such as the word "didjeridu." Try to keep the underlying rhythm and add layers of special effects and vocalizations on top of it. Later, try varying the rhythm by varying the order of the syllables of the word phrase in different ways (e.g. "did did didgeri doo did did doo re doo").

5. Try to become an astute listener. There is a world of rhythm and sounds around you. With careful listening and some practice, sounds that were once annoying sources of distraction become inspiration for relaxing, creative work. This is the magic of the instrument you are playing. Enjoy!

Back to Top

Chapter Four Fourth Lesson

4.1. Double Tonguing -

Double tonguing is a rhythm technique that arranges the beat in couplets by alternate use of the tip and the back of the tongue. The tip of the tongue is rapidly brought down from the roof of the mouth to the floor of the mouth as in pronouncing the word "tuck." Then, the back of the tongue pronounces the word "ka." The resulting word, "Tuck-ka" is repeated to create the couplets. Start slowly until you can clearly hear both parts of each couplet and work up to a rapid tempo. "Tuck-ka, Tuck-ka, Tuck-ka, Tuck-ka."

4.2. Triple tonguing -

Triple tonguing uses the phrase "tuck-it-ta." It is used to create triplet beats. As with double tonguing, start slowly pronouncing each syllable clearly and gradually increase the tempo till you can do it rapidly. "Tuck-It-Ta-Tuck-It-Ta-Tuck-It-Ta."

4.3. Huffing - Huffing is letting the air stream out in puffs or blasts of air using the chest. The result is a rather pronounced vibrato or wavering of the volume. One interesting use of huffing is to apply it to our first overtone note. Play the first overtone note and while sustaining it, vary the airflow by making light "hah-hah-hah" sounds with your breath.

4.4. Overtones again -

By applying the technique of huffing to a long overtone note, a vibrato may be added to the note. Additionally, we can apply the technique learned in the lesson on harmonics to change the characteristics. Higher overtones may be obtain by further tightening the lips so that they buzz at a still higher frequency. As you go up the overtone scale, further breath support is required. By using the tongue and varying the pitch of the overtone notes, a staccato rhythmic effect may be obtained.

Chapter Five Fifth Lesson

5.1. Non-vocal imitations -

You do not have to use your vocal chords to imitate sounds. Some sounds like a Kangaroo hopping or a boomerang flying through the air can be created using just your tongue. A kangaroo hop can be imitated by single tonguing and immediately following the "ta" sound by mouthing the word "boing." A boomerang's flight can be mimicked by rapidly moving the tongue back and forth. Playing the basic drone, place the tip of the tongue just behind the upper front teeth and move it rapidly back and forth. The result is a wavering harmonic which calls to mind the boomerang revolving as it travels through the air.

5.2. Click Sticks -

Click sticks or bilma (sometimes called clap sticks) are a pair of hardwood sticks which are struck against each other to produce a rhythmic beat which can be used to keep time for the didjeridu player. You can purchase Australian clap sticks, substitute clave (which are commonly found at music stores in the percussion area) or make your own out of a pair of hardwood dowels cut to a length of six to eight inches.

I'm going to suggest two approaches to playing with click sticks. The first is to play the rhythm right on each beat of the sticks. In other words, the didjeridu is in synch with the click sticks. The second is to play the didjeridu rhythm just out of synch with the rhythm of the sticks. This can be accomplished by either droning through the beats or "pulling" each note just behind the beat of the sticks. This style affords great opportunities for interesting variations and counter rhythms to be explored.

5.3. Different Didjeridus -

Different instruments have different playing characteristics. Aside from the obvious differences in pitch, there are differences in tonal characteristics and response to various techniques. You may find that an instrument that has a larger diameter is much more suited to vocal effects while a smaller diameter didjeridu may be better suited to fast rhythms. Today, didjeridus are made from a wide variety of materials. I've played didjeridus made from agave flower stalks, PVC pipe, various hardwoods, cardboard tubes, bamboo, metal pipe , ceramics and synthetic resins. I find the rich variety of tonal qualities and playing characteristics a wonderful source of musical experimentation and inspiration.

Chapter Six Some Final Thoughts

All breathing has rhythm. You can emulate the panting of a dog or even the slow respiratory cycle of a plant or tree. In fact, playing for trees and other growing things in the plant kingdom is quite a nice thing indeed! They truly benefit from the carbon dioxide you send their way and they pay us back by producing the life-giving oxygen important to us members of the animal kingdom. Playing the didjeridu outdoors is a wonderful teacher. Not only are there rhythms everywhere, but a world of sounds to imitate. Often, when I play at a park or forest, several birds begin to join in with their songs. Creatures of all kinds gather around. Some just curiously listening and others adding their voices. This is something to be mindful of if you are in an area with dangerous predators. My feeling is that animals attracted to the sounds of a didjeridu playing are merely curious and not likely to be aggressive. That does not mean you should consider not only your situation, but the situation of others who may be in the vicinity. Take in consideration anything in your surrounding that may cause a problem for any visitors or your self. Do you have open food? Are you accompanied by a pet that may be a threat to or endangered by another animal? Common sense is the key here.

My dog and two cats are fascinated by the sounds of the didjeridu. Whenever I play at home, they gather around me. They are content to sit and listen as long as I choose to play. I sometimes perform on the street and have found that dogs on leads are either mildly curious or completely indifferent to the sounds of the didjeridu. But I would caution that all dog owners (myself included) are given to predict their pet's behavior in any circumstance whether they have encountered it before or not. I've seen them jerk their curious pet away from my direction, anxious about some hypothesized reaction to this strange sound. And dogs, being loyal creatures, are very sensitive to their owners feelings of anxiety. I've never had a bad experience, but I see the potential for trouble that is not canine in origin. My personal philosophy about playing outside is not to worry too much about animals, but be wary of humans.

A fun thing to do is to select a stack of CDs or tapes (does anyone remember records?) to play on your stereo, grab your didjeridu, sit down and see how many of your favorite tunes you can accompany. Often, you're in the wrong key and those with perfect pitch will find this exercise painful. Nonetheless, this is a good exercise in listening while playing. I have found that The Doors would have benefited a great deal from a didjeridu player. You may also find a musical group who would be even better if only they had you as a member!

Finally, I try to play with other musicians whenever possible. I don't limit myself to or exclude other didjeridu players. Traditionally, the didjeridu was used primarily to accompany singers and dancers. In traditional aboriginal settings, there may be several singers but only one didjeridu player. Outside of traditional Australian Aboriginal music, however, the didjeridu is played solo, in ensembles of didjeridus and with other instruments.

The interaction between musicians that goes on when we play music together is a great teacher in the art of listening while playing.

Chapter Seven Meditations

As didjeridu players, we are constantly aware of breath patterns and rhythms. Because of this, the didjeridu is an excellent meditation tool. While the didjeridu may be used to meditate, it should not be assumed that such practices have anything to do with its use as such a vehicle in traditional settings. The spiritual life of Australian Aborigines is complex and perhaps beyond the understanding of those of us on the outside. The didjeridu is available to us and we can use it as we wish. In that spirit, I will present a few of my favorite meditations that employ the didjeridu.

7.1 - The pranic sphere :

Sit comfortably in a chair or on the floor in such a manner that you can rest the trumpet end of the didjeridu on the floor. Hold the mouthpiece end to your lips using only one hand (leaving the other hand free for our mudra). Turn your free hand palm up and place the tip of your thumb against the tip of your index finger. Begin circular breathing in a regular and even rhythm.

Now, try to visualize energy coming in from above and below you with each breath. The energy enters a tube running the length of your body as you inhale and travels out through the didjeridu. Once you have this image, try to visualize a small sphere directly in front of you. The energy comes into your body from above and below, travels into the sphere and inflates the sphere much like inflating a balloon.

Now we are going to inflate this sphere to a size that is large enough to encompass our entire body and we are going to do it in seven breaths. For each breath, we will make a sign with our free hand. On the first breath our thumb and first finger are touching. Our sphere begins to expand.

Second breath, thumb and second finger. Our sphere expands to about the size of a basketball. Third breath, thumb and third finger touch, sphere doubles in size. Fourth breath, thumb and little finger. Fifth breath, thumb and first finger again. Sixth breath, thumb touches both the first and second finger. Now the sphere has grown to the size that it can comfortably encompass our entire body. It moves towards us and surrounds us in a warm, protective womb.

Open your palm. Males leave the palm facing upwards. Females turn the palm down. Continue breathing and try to hold this meditation for about ten minutes.

7.2 - Getting small :

Close your eyes, relax and forget about the outside world. Begin playing the basic drone and circular breathing in an even, comfortable pulse of about 10 to 12 breaths per minute. Begin to visualize yourself getting smaller and smaller. It may help to visualize the didjeridu growing larger as you get smaller. Continue to visualize yourself getting smaller until you can begin to feel yourself floating on the air stream. Forget everything but the present and let yourself float with the breaths. It may take some time, but with practice your goal should be to become small enough to float on the breath into the didjeridu and travel down the length of it toward the light at the other end. This may be a bit scary at first. Remember, all you need to do is stop playing and open your eyes. You will be returned to the outside world instantly. If fears come up, do not be courageous. You get no points for courage, only an aversion to playing the didjeridu in this way!

Feelings may well come up with which you may need help. However, if you practice the getting small meditation a little at a time (forgive the obvious pun) you should be able to progress as far as you like with this exercise. Eventually, you may find that you can get small enough to enter a completely different reality. Those who know me well suspect that this is the world I live in! Welcome!

7.3 - Chanting :

Any invocation or prayer that is meaningful to you may be used for this meditation. In the following example, I am going to do a mediation on the number 3. Sit where you can comfortably see a clock. Mentally note the time you begin your meditation and then close your eyes. While droning, mouth the phrase , "one, two, three." The first time do it very slowly. Next do it three times rapidly and follow that by doing it once extremely slowly. Repeat this over and over. You may use your vocal chords to voice the phrase occasionally if you like. Continue this until you become aware that you must stop due to fatigue or boredom. Before opening your eyes, try to estimate the length of time you've been chanting. Now open your eyes and look at the clock. Were you right? Had more or less time passed than you thought? Usually, I think that I've been doing a chanting meditation for about ten minutes when actually thirty minutes have passed.

Chapter Eight Story Telling

Story telling is a time honored tradition in many cultures. One way to incorporate the didjeridu with your story telling is to accompany a narrator by playing softly in the background. Another method is to use the didjeridu to set the mood for your own story. Then tell the story and end with another didjeridu solo. Here I present a little story of my own. See if you can compose a few short passages on the didjeridu at various point in the story that will enhance its telling.

Once, long ago, there lived a young boy who dreamed of the day he would be allowed to take his place amongst the men of the tribe. With each day, he grew stronger in the ways of tracking, combat and his understanding of The Laws of his people.

One night, as most of the tribe lay in their huts dreaming, an elder came to the boy to give him a special and important task. He was to stand watch on this night, without supervision. He would be responsible for guarding the camp and keeping the fire burning all through the cold night. Of course there were other guards out at lookouts around the camp perimeter who would warn of any approaching enemy scouts. But this was truly a task for a man. A sign that soon, he would be initiated as a man. A warrior who would go on the big hunts. A man, ready to take a wife and learn the most secret ways of religious life.

As the night passed and his mates all slept peacefully, the boy began to nod off. He dreamed of being a man. Suddenly, he awoke trembling. The fire was only a faint glow! Fearing his very life, he scrambled to his feet and gathered some dry twigs to throw on the fire. But, in his panic, he threw too much fuel over the dying embers and the glow grew dimmer. Quickly, he knelt to the ground and blew on the faint glow. The embers grew brightly under his breath, but quickly dimmed as he finished his exhalation.

Blowing again and again, the same thing happened every time. The kindling would almost catch, but as his air ran out the fire would die down. The boy thought, "If I could just keep the air flowing long enough for the kindling to catch, I could get the fire going again!"

Looking around for anything which could help him, he spied the old man's Yidaki (didjeridu). He remembered trying to play the instrument as a small boy, but several of the other boys in the tribe had demonstrated much more skill. After a time, he abandoned the instrument as only the best didjeridu player would ever be invited to learn at the feet of the song men and perform at ceremonies.

Lips trembling, he now pointed the Yidaki at the glow and blew a long beautiful note in its direction. This was more efficient and almost enough to get the fire going again. But again, its effect was quickly lost as soon as he paused to take his next breath. By blowing sharply and taking short quick breaths often through his nose, he found he could keep the glow bright but not gain on it. Finally, he puffed out his cheeks at the end of a breath and while squeezing them together, took little sniffs of air through his nose. The movement of his cheeks made a pulsing rhythm as the fire began to breathe to life following his simple beat.

Over the droning sound of the Yidaki, he could faintly hear the sounds of animals preparing for the day in the per-dawn chill. Gradually, he began to try to make the sounds he heard. By the time the kookaburra made its greeting to the morning sun, he was quite adept at making many animal sounds. "Koo Koo Koo Kah kah kah kah kah, he echoed back at his unseen friend. This awoke the entire tribe. The fire was bright and warm as the first rays of light were signaling the start of a new day. By this time, the boy was an expert didjeridu player. Best the tribe had ever heard. And his ability to breathe and play at the same time was drawing much attention, for this technique was not known to even the great musicians in the area. He knew now the scared child who awoke in the middle of the night had died--sacrificed his childhood for the good of all. His mother would not speak with him now until long after he himself took wives to make a family. And his method of "breathing fire" would be his legacy to all the young boys who dream of playing the Yidaki. But only the ones who could breathe in this way dared hope to one day perform with the singers and dancers.

Chapter Nine Suggested Readings

The didjeridu is a wonderful instrument and learning to play it will bring you to a level of appreciation for life that is difficult to describe. To deepen your understanding of it, I feel it helps to learn as much as possible about not only the Australian Aborigine, but the land and animals that sustained them for thousands upon thousands of years.

Our Land is Our Life, Edited by Galarrwuy Yunupingu ISBN 0-7022-2958-X

Published shortly after the 20th anniversary of the Aboriginal Land Rights Act (Northern Territories), this book is a collection of essays on the past, present and future of Land Rights with contributions from leading activists and political figures. It contains a wealth of information on the subject of land rights as well as historical documents, photographs and cartoons form There are prefaces written by the Governor General of Australia and the Chairperson of the Aboriginal and Torres Islander Commission. I am really happy to have found this one. It's the most information in one place and written from the perspective of people who have truely lived these battles.

The Didjeridu: From Arnhem Land to Internet, Edited by Karl Neuenfeldt

Collection of articles which form a study of the didjeridu from a variety of viewpoints. Absolute must reading for the serious didjeriduist. I have read sections of this book many times, taken notes, followed leads from the footnotes and entered into countless debates on the articles contained in this book.

WANDJUCK MARIKA Life Story, as told to Jennifer Isaacs, ISBN 0-7022-2564-9

Perhaps the most important book on this list. Wandjuk was one of Australia's greatest indigenous artists, Yirdaki player, land rights advocate and religious leader. In this book he tells about his people, his land and his dreams. Because of his passing in 1987, this book had to await publication until sufficient time had passed according to the customs of his people and wishes of his family. Published in 1995 by the University of Queensland, this book offers the rare point of view of a traditional Yolngu man on his culture as well as balanda (ours). Highly recommended!

Voices of the First Day Awaking in the Aboriginal Dreamtime, Robert Lawlor
Exhaustive study of the Aboriginal Cosmology, History and Tribal Life. Proceeds from the sale of the book are given to the Denooch Aboriginal Healing Center which assists people of Aboriginal ancestry to free themselves of addictions by using tribal healing methods.
Aboriginal Men of High Degree
A.P. Elkin ISBN 0-89281-421-7

After 200 Years
Photographic Essays of Aboriginal and Islander Australia Today
Edited by Penny Taylor

Australia a Natural History

Book : Howard Ensign Evans and Mary Alice Evans

Australian Aboriginal Paintings
Book by Jennifer Isaacs

Australian Aboriginal Portraits
Book by Charles P. Mountford

Australian Mother and Baby Animals
Book by Carol and Vincent Servently
From the Dreamtime
by Jean A Ellis

I, The Aboriginal
As told to Douglas Lockwood

Letters from a Wild State
Book by James Cowan

My Place
by Sally Morgan

Mysteries of the Dream-Time
The Spiritual Life of Australian Aborigines.
by James Cowan.

Outback
Book by Thomas Keneally

People of the Dreamtime - The Australian Aborigines
Photo essay by Douglas Baglin and David Moore

Shamanism - Archaic Techniques of Ectasy
Mircea Eliade
ISBN 0-691-09827-1

Stradbroke Dreamtime
by Oodgeroo Nunukul (Kathy Walker)

The Aborigine Tradition
Book by James G Cowan
ISNB 1-85230-309-3

The Australian Aborigines
Book : A.P. Elkin

The Red Chief
Book : Ion L. Idriess

The Speaking Land
Ronald M. Berndt and Catherine H. Berndt
ISBN 0 14 01.2072 6

Book : Aboriginal Tales of the Ancestral Powers
Collected by K. Langloh Parker
Edited with commentary by Johanna Lambert

Suggested Listening
Traditional :
Bushfire CD Larrikin Records CDLFRF247
Songs from the Northern Territory Tapes Vol 2 and 3
Goyulan the morning Star An Aboriginal Clan Song Series
from North Central Arnhem   Land. Tape.
Australian Institute of Aboriginal Studies.

Non-Traditional :
David Hudson - CD Woolunda. Rainbow Serpent.
Inlakesh - CD Didjeridu Meditation.
Inlakesh - CD Quantum Dreaming.
Stephen Kent - Tape Songs from the Burnt Earth.
Stephen Kent - CD Landings . City of Tribes Records.

Instructional :
Milkay Mununggurr Hard Tongue Didgeridoo CD
Runtime 34 minutes 15 seconds 47 tracks

At last, an instructional CD on the Yolngu style which covers the essential basics. This is a very basic guide focused on the foundation of the style. The more complicated rhythmic structures found in accompaniment of Yolngu Manikay (songs) are not what this disc is about. It is, rather, a detailed guide to the basic tongue movements used to create those rhythms which are completely different that the movements used in contemporary playing and subtly different than found in Western Arnhem Land playing.

The disc will be of great value to anyone interested in this style who is lacking first hand instruction from the Yolngu, in preparation for such an encounter or as a follow up to time spent in Arnhem Land. Each aspect of tongue movement is demonstrated both by vocal 'singing' of the yirdaki part and playing yirdaki in slow, medium and fast tempo's. Also enlightening are Milkay's explanations of the differences between the parts are demonstrated with the voice and the way they are actually played. Look for that on tracks 42-44.

The disc concludes with some rather nice playing examples that combine all the basic techniques demonstrated on the disc. My only regret is that Milkay didn't 'sing' some of these more complicated patterns so that you could better see how he combines them and transitions between the various techniques when playing more complex patterns.

I want to share some basic things which helped me better utilize this disc. You may discover other little tips as well. Keep in mind, these only helped my perception of my personal progress through the exercises. Your milage may vary and a traditional player who is willing to instruct you is ideal and would trump any of my recommendations. With that out of the way, the first tip I have is to actually sing along with all the examples in all tempos at least once before trying to play along. I just found it's easier to tell if my tongue is really making the desired movements. Second, for me, some of the tongue movements are easier to achieve with my mouth more open than it is while playing didgeridoo. So I continually experimented with singing along with the demonstrations with my mouth more and more conformed to the shape it that will be imposed on it by having the mouthpiece placed on my lips. To the final point of 'singing' the mouth shapes into the didgeridoo without the lips buzzing. Finally, while it is very useful to play right along with Milkay on the disc, I find it very useful to listen through the example, pause the disc and play a bit, then listen some more repeating this process to be sure I am hearing both his example and my attempts clearly. Being able to record yourself will be extremely valuable here, especially if you can listen to the example and then your recorded practice side by side.

Most all the playing examples are in the key of F# with the exception of the overtone examples. Another minor complaint of mine. I rather wish the same instrument was used throughout the entire recording.

Mago Masterclass with Darryl Dikarrna and the White Cockatoo, An introduction to the 'Kunborrk' didjeridu playing style of the Western Arnhem region of Australia. Runtime 48'01".

This is a marvelous instructional recording for so many reasons. The first, and most compelling reason is the way the instruction is put together so that you hear the demonstration of the basic technique first as 'sung' by Darryl, then as a solo didjeridu and finally with the White Cockatoo singing with the didjeridu part. Even better, there is then a track of the White Cockatoo performing the same piece without the didjeridu so that you get to accompany traditional Gunborg (Kunborrk) songs on your own. This is not only a fantastic way to learn, but a rare opportunity to learn somewhat in traditional context the material performed by the White Cockatoo on tour and on their recordings! The Mago or didjeridu that Darryl is playing is in the key of F#.

But there is a treasure of appealing benefits from owning this wonderful recording. Not the least of which is Darryl's narrative. It is quite nice to hear from Darryl in his own language and then in English about his role as a keeper of this tradition, how he came to be a didjeridu player and the history of the instrument with the context of his people. This is extremely rich cultural information that is being shared and is unique to Darryl's family and country. He talks about how it is his job to teach the didjeridu in this way, he inherited it from his Grandfather, how he started to learn to play by listening to him. As someone who met his grandfather, his words are very comforting to me. As Darryl says, it is HIS job and he is doing a remarkable job of it.

The recording quality is stellar, everything is clear and well produced while retaining a really personal 'live' feel. The story of the Mago is presented by David Yirindilli in conversation with Darryl. It is excellent and again a treasure for those interested in the instrument as are the liner notes with contain a lot of insights about the music as well as documenting the tracks.

Alastair Black Earth Tones including "Didgeridoo - A Beginner's Guide

Two CD set. Disc 1 Earth Tones didjeridu Solos 13 tracks Runtime 40:01

Disc 2 Beginner's Guide 1 track Runtime 29:19

Originally released as two separate cassette tapes with the instructional material titled "How to Play the Didgeridoo." Later, a booklet called "Didgeridoo - A beginner's guide." The two were combined in an instructional package when moved to CD. There are some minor differences between the earlier cassette release and the newer double CD release, but the essential content of the instruction remains the same. One difference which is unfortunate, however is that all the lessons on the CD are contained in one track. This makes it difficult to quickly locate a particular part when resuming lessons after a break. The cassette package had considerable written material included which appears to be missing in the CD package, which is regrettable. Much of the information from the Cassette package is covered in narration on the CD, however. Nonetheless, it is a good beginner's instructional tool. There was some political reasons why this CD is not as available to US customers as it once was which I will explain later as well as try to source where US customers can obtain a copy if they desire one. Alastair produced one of the first instructional audio packages available and of those early ones, it still holds up well against many who have come after.

Basically, Alastair has divided learning into two major divisions. Basic sound production comes first, with much attention to animal impersonations and sounds effects, changes in blowing pressure, tongue positions, diaphragm pressure and cheek movements. This is good detailed instruction which gives the student much to practice before beginner the laborious process of learning to circular breath as well as develops the needed strength and techniques to successfully attempt the circular breathing lessons.

The circular breathing instruction here is broken down in to eight steps, almost painfully detailed. However, for people who find this process mystifying, this rather scientific approach to teaching it may be rewarding where simpler instructions may have failed them. In my experience, the main successes in circular breathing mainly come from persistence and practice. This step by step method will work if given the students complete attention and effort. And many will find it very helpful.

As for negatives on this package I can only call attention to a few omissions. Only one method of circular breathing is taught. Not much of a negative since once you've mastered the cheek squeezed method, you can certainly refine and advance your circular breathing. In this method, breath is always fitted to rhythm which is quite a common starting point for non-traditional learners anyway and the recording supplied in the collection, "Earth Tones" clearly demonstrates all rhythms and techniques taught in the course - which is excellent for the learner. Many newer packages cover more ground, however many, if not most do not. As for the earlier reference to 'politics', I perhaps such have said business. A United States distributer aggressively obtained large distributions for Alastair's products in the US to the point of practically having an exclusive on them. Once the distribution grew to nicely profitable levels, he quickly recorded his own instructional CD, dumped Alastair's product and filled all his customers orders with his own. Business is business I guess....

What I find sad here is that this literally thousands of people around the world learned to play using this product and it was targeted for extinction in the USA for reasons of increasing profit rather than providing a better product. The result is a lesser product by a less experienced player and teacher. One of the reasons I've undertaken this review and documentation of all available instructional products (and I will be hitting videos, books and booklets as well) is to show how many choices for the beginner there truly are out there as well as how many resources the didjeridu instructor has to draw from.

Didgeridoo Made Easy A Beginner's Guide with Ash Dargan

2 discs disc one English and German Runtime 65:02

disc two French and Spanish Runtime 65:23

Another relatively recent product, this package features multi language narration as well as a multi language booklet which covers every track on the CD. First of all, I really like a package that includes written material. It makes it so much easier to quickly refer to specifics of any lesson between listens to and practice with the audio material. Additionally, the written material includes brief information on the history of the instrument, how they are made, the geographic regions of origin, playing styles, instrument care, instrument types and answers to frequently asked questions.

There are basically eight steps in the lesson plan starting with production of the basic drone, using the tongue, playing with syllables (mouth shapes), creating basic rhythms, circular breathing, breath exercises, animal sounds and finally some additional rhythm examples.

Also really good is the presentation of each sound first using the voice, then through buzzing lips and finally through the didgeridoo is a great way to learn. This course is very consistent in this which means the learner really knows what to expect ever step of the way. The narrations are quite clearly done as well.

The section on circular breathing is also somewhat original. For people who are having trouble getting the circular breathing, it is always worth while to get a different approach to the technique. This one involves actually spitting water down your didgeridoo so be prepared for some major "leakage" at the bottom of your didge. At minimum, I would suggest playing over a towel or perhaps a bucket for this one! Circular breathing is not broken down in as many steps as in Alastair Black's method. This section could probably have been expanded a bit to explain the role of the tongue, cheeks and diaphragm. However, in context with the rest of the learning material presented, it is an appropriate treatment of the subject. A down fall of many instructors is to over emphasis or make too much of circular breathing on the instrument. Most people take some amount of time and experimentation to get it after all. There is so much more to playing the instrument than circular breathing.

Sleep Apnea and the Didjeridu

In December of 2005, the British Medical Journal published a study called , " Didgeridoo playing as alternative treatment for obstructive sleep apnoea syndrome : Randomized controlled trial." News of the paper spread through various media and very soon after adds from didgeridoo shops started appearing throughout cyberspace using tag lines like , "Snoring? Play the didgeridoo!" For several years I've been in contact with various people who are suffering from sleep apnea and I have cautiously encouraged them to try it. I think it's time to discuss the study a bit, How to use this information and what is reasonable or not reasonable to expect from adding didgeridoo playing as an adjunct to therapy for sleep apnea.

The first good step is to read the original study, if you haven't already. Here is the link to the original study and I would encourage readers to read the follow up comments as well as some of them raise some very important considerations. I'll talk a bit about those when I cover expectations. Here then, is the link to the article in the BMJ that started it all :

http://www.bmj.com/content/332/7536/266.full

The study doesn't really give a clear answer to the question of how playing the didgeridoo improves upper airway flow during sleep. I suspect that it the answer has probably more to do with the strengthening of muscles that surround the soft tissues of the upper airway and less to do with sound vibration. Though I do not completely discount sound frequencies playing a role here.

There are several things to consider about the study that aren't mentioned in most of the media releases, videos and references to it. The study used a fairly small sample size, which is an important thing to consider before making broad statements about the results. Also, very often when we have good studies on something, the results are not reproducible in subsequent trials. And as of this writing, I'm not aware of anyone trying to repeat the study. Nor would I hold my breath waiting for one (sorry, bad pun that!). If we were talking about a new drug for sleep apnea, studies would be plentiful. Funding for clinical trials of exercise techniques is considerably less appealing to private funders. A follow up survey at five years with the participants would be a golden opportunity to see what the long term benefits of this may be as well. Perhaps this has been done and not yet published.

"But, I've been playing the didgeridoo for years and I snore!"

I know! So do I and believe me, I've roomed with lots of didgeridoo players and heard them snore as well. But perhaps we haven't been practicing the techniques we did in the beginning when we were first learning to circular breath and initially using the muscles involved for the first time. Now, circular breathing to us is pretty much done effortlessly. Also, as we go along as players all the muscles around the lips have developed and practiced the lip buzzing techniques to a degree that we probably don't use the techniques we first learned to achieve a drone while breathing in through the nose. Bounced breaths place heavy emphasis on the diaphragm and are performed quickly. If you watched the video and listened to the playing style, these players are more "airplane" style players than staccato rhythm machines. Score one in the column that it is the circular breathing that provides the benefit vs just sound vibration.

If it was just sound therapy alone, just using the right frequency instrument would produce the desired effect. Still, can't rule out that it is the combination of sound frequencies and circular breathing that produced the improvement in this group. Thus, I recommend anyone wanting to use didgeridoo to improve sleep, decrease snoring and hopefully also periods of apnea, try to follow the example of the study as closely as possible. If you are already playing, you're going to devote some of your practice time to going back to basics as it were, circular breathing away for 25 or 30 minutes a day. Good time to work on tone, harmonics, breath support and perhaps a little meditation.

"So how do I try it?"

In order to secure the best chance of a positive result I believe one should follow the procedures used in the study as closely as possible. It is the best model we have of successful use of the instrument in this application so far. Why not try to reproduce the same steps used in the study as closely as possible? I don't go so far as replicating the exact instruments used in the study group. But if you have access to the same materials that they used, I say go for it. In my opinion, approximating the basic dimensions and tonal frequencies of the instruments described in the study is probably good enough. The instruments used were 130 cm long (51.2"), a diameter of 4cm (~1.57") and a mouthpiece diameter of between 2.8 and 3.2 cm. What I suggest as a good enough copy is schedule 40 white PVC 1.5" pipe cut to a length of approximately 51" with a hand molded beeswax mouth piece that is 1 to 1.25 inches in diameter.

If your shopping for a ready made instrument, a slide didjeridu that can play in the key of C or a wooden, bamboo or agave didgeridoo which plays in the key of C. Just for the purpose of staying as close as possible to the kind of back pressure and playing response of the instruments used in the study, one would do well to consider a nice agave or bamboo instrument that plays in the key of C. Would an instrument with stronger back pressure do just as well or better? Short answer: I don't know. There is some evidence that actually an instrument with higher resistance (back pressure) may be better. There have been studies on sleep apnea and oboe (a higher back pressure instrument) for example. But if the goal is to get the same results as the participants in the study did, I favor duplicating the study instruments as closely as possible.

Once you have an instrument, time to get to work! In the study, the participants were given an initial lesson on tone production and taught to maintain tone for 20 to 30 second intervals. They worked on this for a period of one week and then received another lesson from a didgeridoo instructor on the basics of circular breathing. After four weeks, the instructor repeated the lesson and finally again at eight weeks. The didgeridoo students were asked to practice at home at least 20 minutes per day five days a week. Which begs the question, "do I need to find a didgeridoo teacher?" Of course you can. Is it absolutely necessary? People have different learning styles. Some people are quite comfortable learning from printed manuals, some need to hear the information to learn it, and some people are very visual and learn best from observation. But most of us are some combination of all of the above. There is a wealth of instructional material available in the form of audio recordings, books and video. A large chunk of it is free. Having an instructor is a great way to get good feedback about your playing. But for many, a simple audio CD may give enough information and examples to learn the basics of circular breathing.

You're going to play at least 20 minutes a day, five days a week. In the study, participants averaged 25.3 minutes per day for an average of 5.9 days per week. And, if the study is our gold standard, it's going to be some weeks before you see some if any results for your effort. The good news here is that this type of playing does have some benefits aside from potentially improving your breathing during sleep. It is relaxing. It should calm you (especially if you try not to be overly self critical or impatient during the learning process. I did a little experiment on myself. For two weeks I measured my blood pressure before and after playing the didgeridoo for 20 minutes in a calm setting. What I found in my simple exercise was that my systolic and diastolic blood pressure readings were consistently about 2 to 5 mm/Hg lower after playing. I'd love someone to do a clinical trial on the effects on blood pressure by didgeridoo playing because my little uncontrolled experiment makes me suspect there is a good chance that for some people at least, didgeridoo playing may play a role in blood pressure. But that's for another conversation.

How will I know if it's doing anything?

Remember it's going to take weeks to months to notice an improvement. Like most holistic approaches to health care, it may be quite subtle and it may only address part of the overall picture. You'll definitely want to confront as many of the risk factors associated with obstructive sleep apnea that are within your control. That is to not only just add didgeridoo playing to your daily routine, but strive to attain your ideal body weight, quit or at least reduce your consumption of tobacco and limit your consumption of alcohol.

I would suggest keeping some kind of journal for a few months. This will serve to document any improvements in sleep quality, decrease in daytime drowsiness and changes in overall health. It will also give you feedback that helps you stay on task. Record the amount of time you spent playing the didgeridoo that day and any notes or comments about the practice session you feel important. Make an entry at least once a day that reflects the issues which concern you about sleep apnea. For example, if you are in a relationship and your partner is willing to contribute to the journal, a daily note on how much you are snoring would be great. Trust me, they will have noticed your snoring! Also record the things that you feel affect your health goals. Blood pressure, if you can measure it at home. Weight reduction, if you are fighting that battle. Number of cigarettes you've smoked if you are a smoker. Number of alcoholic beverages you've consumed in the past twenty four hours if you think that is something you need to monitor as well. But most important, a quick note on how you feel. Did you wake up with a headache? Have you had trouble concentrating on simple tasks, remembering appointments, or even doing the daily crossword? How is your energy? A journal like this can really be of value when you are trying to make life style changes and it can also really help you to give your doctor a good solid history of what's going on with you.

Periodically, review your journal and look for trends. For example, on days that you do not have any alcohol did you feel more rested and alert the next day? On days you had the fewest or no cigarettes? If your weight is going down, is your blood pressure also going down? Since most of the indicators of sleep apnea outside a controlled environment like a sleep study lab are in fact subjective a journal will be very helpful as you look at your overall quality of life. Playing the didgeridoo is an inexpensive, enjoyable activity that is available. One which I think has many potential benefits to the player. One benefit may well be improved ventilation during sleep which translates to improved quality of life.

Glossary

In talking with didjeridu players as well as reading about the instrument, there is a wonderful amount of jargon that has emerged over the years which you rarely see defined or explained. This is my brief attempt to explain some of the terms which are commonly thrown around in forums, articles and books about playing the didjeridu.

Airplane style - Sometimes called Balinda style, refers to the perception of non-traditional and non-rhythmic plays styles which sometimes sounds like an airplane flying over head.

Agave Didj - didjeridu made from the flower stalk of the agave plant. Extremely light weight compared with hardwood and even bamboo didjeridus.

Back pressure - The resistance felt when blowing into the didjeridu.

Balinda Yolngu word for non-Aboriginal peoples. Probably refers to the word Hollander which dates back to early contact with Dutch explorers in Arnhemland. Balanda style didjeridu playing is a references to non-traditional playing styles.

Bare back - When players talk about an instrument that can be played 'bare back' they mean that the diameter and shape of the mouth end of the didjeridu is appropriate without adding beeswax or any other type of mouthpiece.

Barky Slang name applied to didjeridus that retain a portion of the original bark on them, usually toward the end.

Bilma - Yolngu word for clapsticks.

Bounced Breath - Breath taken during a rapid compression of the diaphragm or "gutslap".

Cheek slap - Rapid squeeze of either both or one cheek producing a short sharp rhythmic beat in the drone pattern.

Bungul - Yolgnu word for ceremony. Most often used to describe the associated playing style.

Chording - Using to voice to hum or sing notes in harmony with the fundamental drone note.

Circular Breathing - Technique of breathing in through the nose while simultaneously producing a lip buzzing drone sound usually by squeezing the air contained in the mouth through the lips during the inhalation.

Didjeridu, Didgeridoo and other variations of spellings - Probably Australian English slang for the Aboriginal instrument which you are learning to play. There are several words for the instrument depending on the language spoken in the region. The most common is the Yolngu word Yirdaki which is descriptive of the instruments of Eastern Arnhem Land and associated with those playing styles. In other areas, the playing style and instrument styles differ as well as the appropriate name of the instrument. Maku (sometimes spelled Magu or Margot) usually more cylindrical shaped than the more conical shaped yirdaki.

Didj-box - Created by Dr. Marco Johnson, and ingenious method of routing the airflow to make an instrument short enough to toss in your suitcase, but plays the same note as an instrument perhaps four to five feet in length. Great practice, travel instrument to have!

Didj-flute - Variation on the didj-box with finger holes allowing you to change pitches while playing just like a simple flute.

Didj-healing (or didj massage) Practice of playing the didjeridu over various parts of the body for the effect the sound vibrations have. Feels great!

Double tonguing - alternately striking the tip and back of the tongue against the roof of the mouth to create couplets, as in doog-gaa or too-kaa

Euc - Short for eucalyptus, refers to a didjeridu hallowed out by termites.

Gut slap - A sudden increase in pressure by compressing the abdominal muscles and pronouncing a hard "H" consonant with or without vocalization.

Jaw Drop - A technique with lowers the pitch of the drone by lowering the jaw slightly while keeping the lips buzzing.

NEAL - Northeastern Arnhem Land often used in reference to either the origin of an instrument or the associated playing style.

Overtone - In most cases refers to the notes reached by playing with the lips held in a tighter position than the fundamental basic note of the drone. Usually between and octave and a 12th above the fundamental note. On some instruments it's possible to reach up to the third overtone or in rare cases depending on the player further. Sometimes referred to as "trumpeting" or tooting.

Slide-Didj or Didj-bone - Originally invented by Charlie McMahon , an instrument constructed of at least two pieces of plastic pipe arranged such that the the outside diameter of one pipe fits into the inside diameter of the other allowing the player to create different pitches. Works just like a slide trombone.

Retroflex Tongue - Tongue position created when the underside of the tongue contacts the roof of the mouth just behind the top row of teeth.

Triple Tonguing - Rapidly striking the tip, back and then tip of the tongue to form triplets as in "tuck-It-Tah."

Side Saddle - Along with the expression bare back, one of the two equine metaphors on the subject of mouthpieces and the people who love them I have heard. This refers to the practice of orienting the mouthpiece slightly or completely off center on the lips either to the left or the right. Many people find it easier to get good quality sound using this method. It does however make some techinques a bit more challenging, for example overtones. However with practice, most such difficulties can be over come. A long time ago, I polled several players on this subject and two of the responses were, I think, quite telling. Both came from fully experienced musicians and top notch didj players. The first was short and sweet, "I play with the mouthpiece centered in the front, for control." Fair enough, the player feels he has the most control of his instrument playing as most brass players do, with the mouth piece centered just below the nose. The second response, "depends on the size of the mouthpiece, if it is small I play with the mouthpiece at the center of my lips, but for larger mouthpieces I tend to play with it off to one side." My experiments bear out that if the mouthpiece is larger than 1.25 I find it much easier to play it from the corner of my mouth, using one cheek to seal some of the diameter.

Split and Hollow Didj - refers to the method of construction. A piece of hard wood or tree limb or whatever is split in half, the two halves hollowed out (usually using a wood router) and then the two halves are glued back together to create a hollow tube.

Tongue trill - Air movement across a relaxed tongue allows the tongue to flutter or trill. Usually the tip of the tongue, though the back of the tongue may also be trilled as well.

Tourist Didj - Refers to instruments made primarily for sales in gift shops as keepsakes, often have elaborate but not traditional artwork. Usually not great playing characteristics since they aren't produced for that, but occasionally then can be quite playable.

Travel Didj - instrument that is easy to travel with for practice. Some people carry their slide didjs or didjboxes. I've also seen plastic didjs that 'break down' into three or more parts which can be reassembled for playing.

Yirdaki (Yiḏaki) - Yolngu word for didjeridu.

Yolngu Aboriginal people of Northeastern Arnhem Land.

Yolngu Matha, group of languages spoken by the Yolngu.

WAL - Western Arnhem Land, frequently seen in reference to the origin of a didjeridu or the style of playing from that part of Australia.

Made in United States
Troutdale, OR
12/01/2023

15196459R00033